RENT

VOCAL SELECTIONS

Cover photos: Amy Guip

Interior photos: Joan Marcus

ISBN 978-0-7935-7229-8

HAL•LEONARD®
CORPORATION

For all works contained herein:
Unauthorized copying, arranging, adapting, recording or public performance is an infringement of copyright.
Infringers are liable under the law.

68   Another Day

34   Halloween

39   I'll Cover You

55   One Song Glory

22   Out Tonight

10   Rent

46   Santa Fe

63   Seasons of Love

92   Take Me or Leave Me

81   What You Own

29   Without You

100 Your Eyes

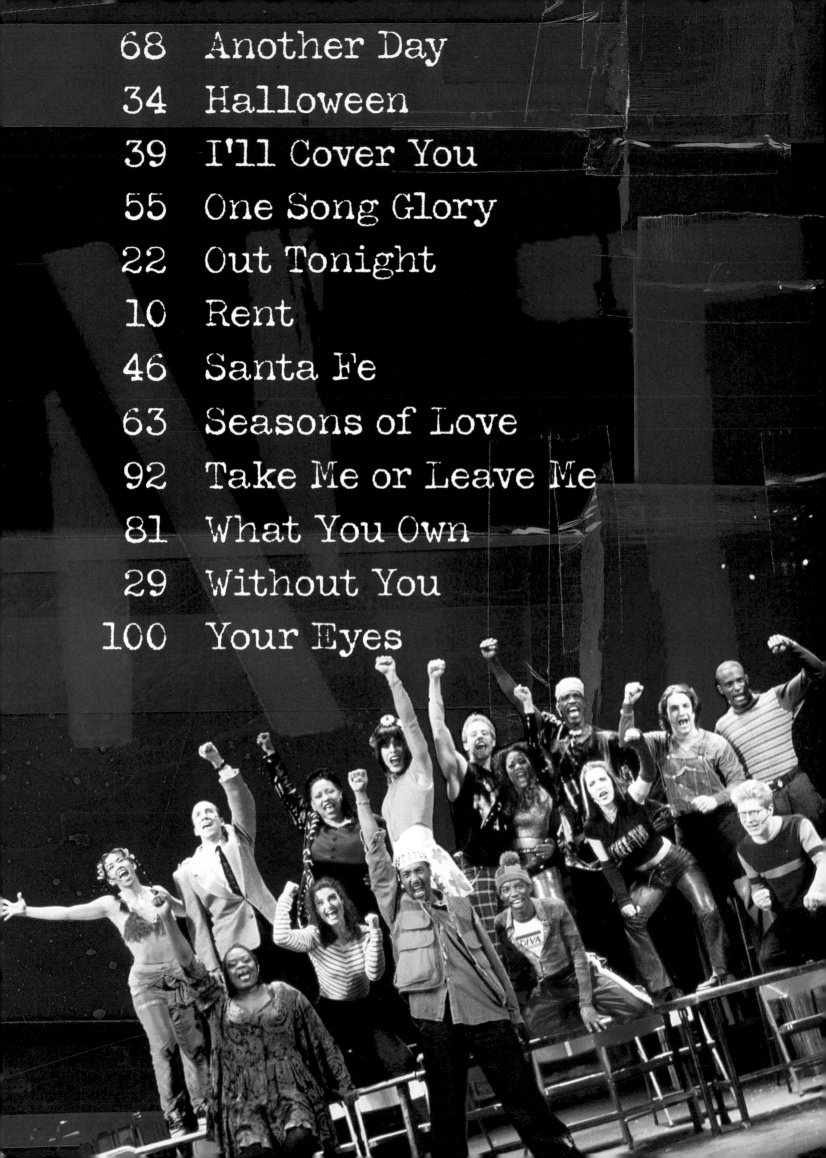

Jonathan Larson

February 4, 1960 - January 25, 1996

Jonathan Larson spent the greater part of his life working toward success in the theater. For most of his last fourteen years, he supported himself as a waiter while struggling to combine modern music with the drama of

live theater; theater that would appeal to his generation and to those that would follow. While he had plans for much more, RENT was the culmination of those efforts.

Jonathan did not live to see RENT open Off Broadway. He did not read the rave reviews or see the limousines lined up in front of the small theater...did not watch his show move to Broadway and to theaters around the country...was not able to accept the Pulitzer Prize and Tony® Awards he earned or to revel in the presence of a Broadway audience that was joyously yelling and applauding.
He never had the pleasure of being engulfed in the electrifying excitement that is present when RENT is on the stage.

His sudden, unexpected death on the day before his dream came true is the stuff of tragedy.

But Jonathan's was a magnificent talent and he left us a magnificent gift. He left us a show that is of our time — and of all time. A show that speaks in both words and music to the specific issues of today and to the timeless problems that humankind has faced through all eternity. A show that gives us another way to look at things. A show that teaches love — not fear.

It is an enormous gift which, happily, is reaching, touching and changing thousands of lives.

It is his legacy; his gift to us and to our children and to our children's children. Enjoy it.

Photo: Richard Lee

Rent

Words and Music by
JONATHAN LARSON

Bright Rock

How do you doc - u - ment _ real life when real life's

Out Tonight

Words and Music by
JONATHAN LARSON

24

Without You

Words and Music by
JONATHAN LARSON

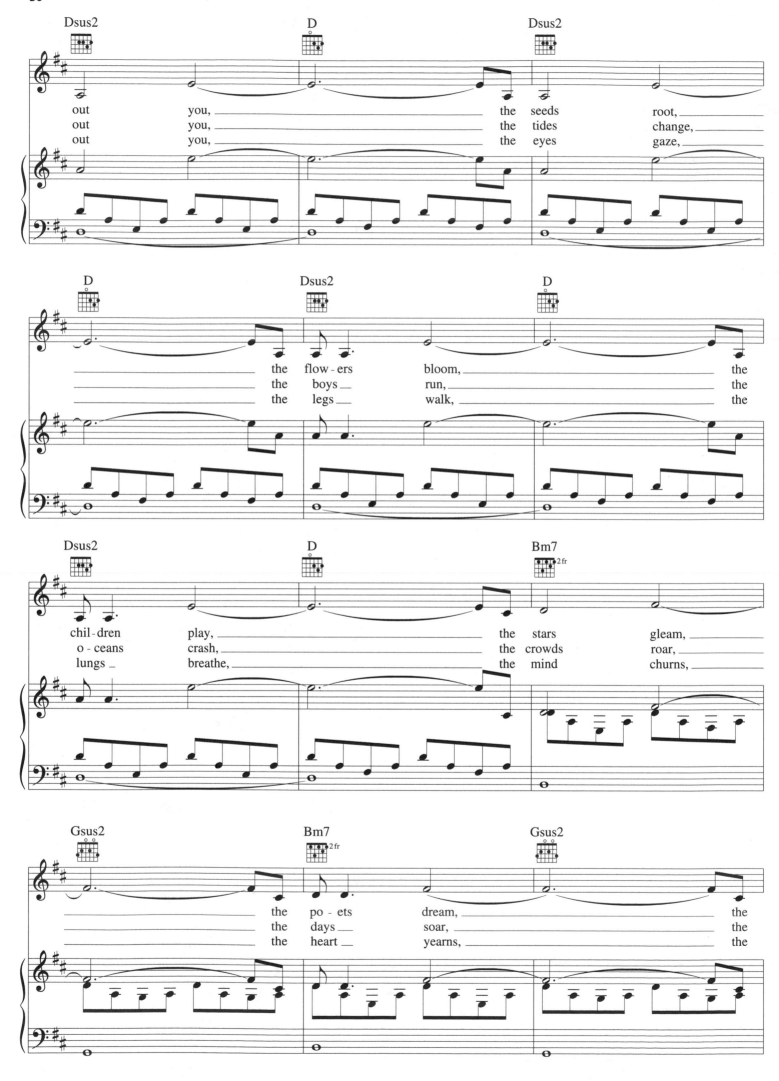

Halloween

Words and Music by
JONATHAN LARSON

I'll Cover You

Words and Music by
JONATHAN LARSON

Moderate Light Rock

Male 1: Live in ___ my house, I'll be ___ your shel - ter; ___ just pay ___ me back with one thou - sand kiss - es. ___ Be my lov - er, ___ and I'll cov - er ___ you. ___

Santa Fe

Words and Music by
JONATHAN LARSON

One Song Glory

Words and Music by
JONATHAN LARSON

Seasons of Love

Words and Music by
JONATHAN LARSON

Another Day

Words and Music by
JONATHAN LARSON

Moderately bright

What You Own

Words and Music by
JONATHAN LARSON

Don't breathe too deep, don't think all day. _____ Dive in - to work,

drive the oth - er way. _____

Take Me or Leave Me

Words and Music by
JONATHAN LARSON

97

Your Eyes

Words and Music by
JONATHAN LARSON